This book belongs to

____

QUEEN BEE

a collection of short stories

Color Edition

Printed in the United States of America

Color Edition
v. 3.1.0

All About® Learning Press, Inc.
615 Commerce Loop
Eagle River, WI 54521

ISBN 978-1-935197-77-5

Stories:

Marie Rippel:	"Ruben and the Secret Gift" - "Mrs. Marvel's Garden" "Storm in the North" - "In My Backpack" "Pumpkin and the Kitten" - "Life on *The Blue Whale*" "Wild Rice Harvest" - "Rawhide"
Renée LaTulippe:	"Dragon in the Wagon" - "Under the Carpet" "Oh, Brother!" - "Cricket's Picnic" - "Queen Bee"

Illustrations:

Donna Goeddaeus:	"Ruben and the Secret Gift" - "Mrs. Marvel's Garden" "Storm in the North" - "Dragon in the Wagon" "In My Backpack" - "Pumpkin and the Kitten" "Oh, Brother!" - "Cricket's Picnic" "Wild Rice Harvest" - "Rawhide"
Dave LaTulippe:	"Under the Carpet" - "Life on *The Blue Whale*" "Queen Bee"

Contributors:	Samantha Johnson, Jon Stenschke, Rebecca Webber
Cover Design:	Dave LaTulippe
Page Layout:	Dave LaTulippe, Andy Panske
Colorization of Stories:	Donna Goeddaeus

Queen Bee: a collection of short stories is part of the *All About® Reading* program.

For more books in this series, go to www.AllAboutReading.com.

To the reader—

may you be inspired
to embark on
your own adventures

Contents

Ruben and the Secret Gift

Ruben

“What’s in this box?” Ruben said to Mom.

“You’ll have to open it to see,” Mom said.

“Is it for me? Is it from you?”

“Your name is on the tag. But it’s not from me. Open it!” said Mom.

Ruben took the gift out of the box.

"A hand lens!" he said. "And here's a note."

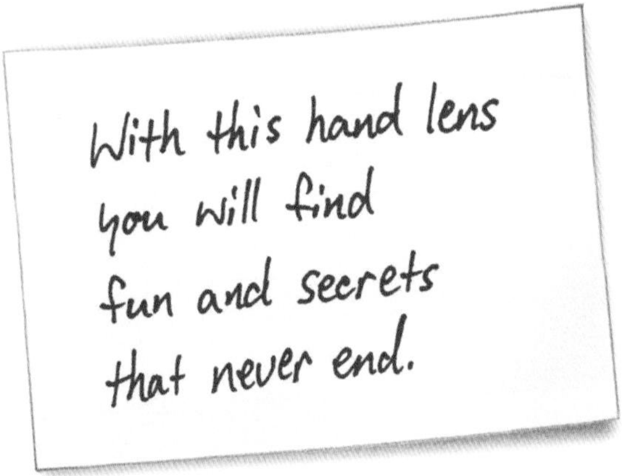

"Is this from Dad?" Ruben said.

"I can't tell. It's a secret," said Mom.

“This is the best gift ever!”

“Yes, I think you’ll have fun with it.”

"Mom, can I have some paper? I will keep notes on what I see under the lens," said Ruben.

Mom gave Ruben a notepad.

Ruben slid the hand lens and the notepad into his bag. "I'll go into the desert to find fun and secrets that never end, just like the note said!"

"Fine," said Mom. "But be home by six. My sister Zumac and her husband will be here, and Don is not a fan of the desert. If we can, let's make him feel at home."

"OK, I won't be late!" said Ruben.

"Here is a sandwich for your lunch," said Mom.

Ruben stuck the sandwich in his bag. With a wave, he left for the desert.

“What will a cactus be like under my hand lens?” Ruben said to himself.

"I see an insect that has taken shelter in the spines. Hold on while I add you to my notepad!"

"Here is a desert aster! I'll get close to it with my lens."

Ruben made a note. *"Under the lens, the aster seems to glitter."*

"I see a jackrabbit! I'll add him to my notepad."

“A killdeer! To keep her eggs safe, the killdeer pretends she has a broken wing. She thinks I’ll chase her and won’t see the nest in the sand,” said Ruben.

“I’ll add this to my notes.”

After a while, it was time for lunch. Ruben sat in the shade of a desert plant.

As he ate his sandwich, Ruben's mind went back to the hand lens. Who gave him the gift?

"Let me think. Whoever gave me the hand lens must have left fingerprints behind. I can check for fingerprints!"

Ruben *did* see fingerprints on the hand lens.

"But which prints are mine and which prints aren't?"

"Those fingerprints on the plastic must be mine. But I see a big fingerprint on the glass—and it's not mine."

He came up with a plan.

"I'll use tape to lift the fingerprint from the glass. Then I'll stick the fingerprint onto paper so I can see it better."

Ruben ran home. He got some black dust and tape.

Rap, rap, rap.

It was Zumac and Don!

Mom ran to meet them. Ruben was close behind.

"Zumac!" said Mom as she gave her sister a big hug. "I'm so glad to see you. It has been so long!"

"And I'm glad to see you! But Don is not so glad to be in this hot desert."

"I won't be in the desert for long," said Don. "I'll melt!"

"Well, sit and relax while I get dinner," said Mom.

"Can I take your fingerprints?" said Ruben to Don and Zumac.

"Ruben!" said Mom. "Don and Zumac just got here!"

"It's OK. It will be fun," said Don.

Ruben held Don's and Zumac's fingerprints next to the print that came from the hand lens. The fingerprints told him the gift was from …

… Don!

"This hand lens is the best gift I ever got. Thank you!" said Ruben.

Then Ruben slid his notepad from his bag and gave it to Don and Zumac. "This is a gift for both of you!"

Don's gaze went from one sheet of the notepad to the next. It was a side of the desert that Don had never seen before.

The cactus spines. The insects. The asters. The jackrabbit and the killdeer. The shimmer of the desert sun.

"Ruben, I need to thank *you*! You just gave me the gift of the desert," said Don.

The End

Mrs. Marvel's Garden

WIND CHIMES
for Sale!
Mrs. Marvel's
Garden Art

I met Mrs. Marvel last summer at an art sale in the park. She sold wind chimes that she made from old jars, bells, and scraps of tin.

The chimes made a soft "clink, clink, clink" as the wind went by.

"Do you like wind chimes?" Mrs. Marvel said. Her smile was kind.

"Yes! I cannot see well, so it helps if I feel them."

"You can make one to take home," she said. She strung pots and silverware on strings.

She gave me a brush and I made stripes and zigzags on the pots.

"Such fine art!" Mrs. Marvel said.

The next week, I went to Mrs. Marvel's Garden.

A rock held open the garden gate, which was made from an old bed frame.

"I like to go in bare feet," Mrs. Marvel said.

I set my socks on the bench with hers.

The path was made of warm, flat stones and thick green moss.

Plants sprung from pots, planters, and baskets.

I bent over to feel the plants.

Mrs. Marvel said the names of the plants as I felt them.

"Stem roses."
"Wintergreen."
"Hens and chicks."
"Rock cress."
"Mums."

An old bike had grape vines on it.

Peppers and greens sat in old tires.

I let the cucumber vine twist on my finger like a ring.

An old milk crate held a big fern under a tree. A frog hid under a frond.

A rope swing hung from a thick branch.

Mrs. Marvel broke off part of a plant.

"What is this?" She held it up to my nose.

"Mint! I smell mint!"

"Yes! It is mint!"

Mrs. Marvel got the hose.

“The plants feel dry. Let’s give them a drink.”

"The garden is home to critters, too, like bees and this butterfly," Mrs. Marvel said. "And peek under here."

"Rabbits!"

Mrs. Marvel and I made a star for the garden gate with twigs and twine.

I like to visit Mrs. Marvel's Garden!

The End

Storm in the North

It is winter in the north. A big storm has left a fresh blanket of deep, white fluff. The forest is silent and still.

A pup sets off on a hike to see what he can find.

He meets three otters at the river. The otters slide from the top of the hill.

Splash!

The river is cold, but the otters don't mind. It is fun to see them romp on this brisk morning.

The pup trots past the otters and meets a shy muskrat.

The rodent sits on the shore and munches on a dry plant.

When he sees the pup, he dives under the bank to a secret home.

Plop!

A glob drops from a tree onto the pup. It's cold!

He shakes it off and stares up to see a finch on a frozen twig.

The finch sings a song of winter cheer. Tweet! Tweet!

The pup spots a hole under an old tree stump. He peeks in to see a stash of acorns.

A chipmunk is deep in her winter sleep. Sh! The pup creeps back to his path. He won't wake her!

The pup finds fresh tracks. What can it be?

A herd of deer stands on the hilltop. The deer spot the pup.

Stomp! Snort!

Then the deer dash into the forest.

A bobcat springs up from behind an evergreen tree.

The bobcat runs after a plump vole. The vole darts back and forth and then vanishes into a deep drift.

The pup barks and the bobcat jumps back into the pines.

As the sun sinks behind the trees, the pup starts for home.

It's fun to meet winter critters in the north!

The End

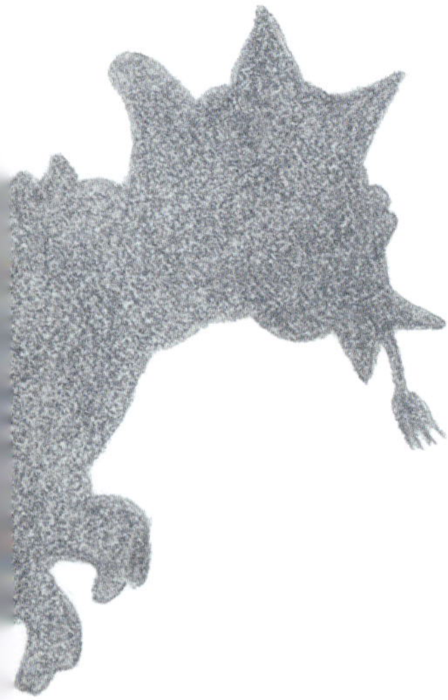

Dragon in the Wagon

Sal likes art.
Sal likes dragons.
Sal will make a dragon with a green pen!

Sal grabs his wagon. He will go find a green pen to make a dragon.

Is that a pen over there in the corner?

ROLL, ROLL, ROLL! Sal pulls his wagon to the corner.

It's just a skate with a broken wheel. Sal shrugs and drops the skate in his wagon.

But there is no green pen
to put in the wagon
to make a dragon.

Sal thinks. What is the best spot to find a green pen? The bathtub!

SLIP, SKID, SLIDE! The wagon slips on the slick tiles.

What is in the bathtub? Three lemons! Who put lemons in the bathtub?

And what is this on the sink? A hand puppet!

Sal snorts and shrugs and stacks them in his wagon.

But where will he find a green pen
to put in the wagon
to make a dragon?

Sal stops to think.

CRASH, CLANK, CLUNK! Sal and his wagon clack to the basement.

There *must* be a pen here somewhere!

Sal finds
a picnic basket,
a brass horn,
a rubber chicken,
a red rocket,
five buttons,
and a plastic fork.

He stacks them in his wagon …

but there is *still* no green pen
to put in the wagon
to make a dragon.

Sal thinks for a moment. He has a snack of plum cake. (Plum cake helps him think.)

Before he can finish his cake, Sal jumps up. There is one more spot to check for a green pen!

Sal stacks the plate of plum cake in his wagon and …

BUMP, THUMP, BUMP! Sal's wagon bumps on the steps to the yard.

Sal stomps over the grass. He checks behind a bush. No pen.

He checks under a rock. No pen.

He checks in the barn. There's no pen, but Sal finds a bull!

Sal pushes hard. The bull will not go.

Sal pulls hard. The bull will not go.

What can Sal do to get the bull in the wagon?

Sal puts grass in the wagon and the bull jumps in.

Sal has
a big black bull,
a plate of plum cake,
a plastic fork,
five buttons,
a red rocket,
a rubber chicken,
a brass horn,
a picnic basket,
a hand puppet,
three lemons,
and a skate with a broken wheel.

The wagon is full, but there is no green pen to make a dragon.

Sal slumps by his wagon. He just can't find a green pen.

But what is this?

There is a dragon! A dragon is in the wagon!

ROLL, SLIP, THUMP, CLANK!

Sal strolls off with his wagon full of dragon.

The End

Under the Carpet

What do you do when it is dark
and you see a place in the center
of your carpet ...

and that place has a lump?

Do you push it and pull it?
Do you put a jar over it?
Do you poke it with a stick?
Do you bolt from bed and stomp on it?
Do you race to get your mom or dad?

Or do you just peek at it twice
and then go back to sleep?

I will tell you what *I* do.

I pull the sheet up to my face and see if I can tell what is under that carpet!

Is it a spider that scampers under
my rug?

Is it a chimp on the run?

Is it seven mice that march in a line?

Is it a herd of lost deer?

Or is that lump a stork that takes shelter from the storm?

No, it is none of those things.

Then is it my sister with her big brass trumpet?

Is it a flock of sheep?

Is a robber here to take my robot?

Did my dad park his jeep under my rug?

Or is it the king from my chess game who hides from his queen?

No, it is none of those things.

Is it a pile of red beets from
the garden?

Or is it an old ox frozen in ice?

Is it a duck that needs a safe place
to molt?

Is it a hive full of bees that wish to
sting me?

Or is that lump a wigwam in which a tribe makes its home?

Just what *is* that lump under my carpet?

I *wish* that the lump was …

… a deep, dark cave.

… a basket full of soft kittens.

… a rock from space in the shape of a star.

… a whale that I can keep as a pet.

But the lump is not a spider or a robber or a king or a stork.

It is not a cave or a kitten or a rock or a whale.

No, I remember what it is!

It is just the sandwich from lunch that I forgot to finish!

I roll over and go back to sleep.

The End

In My Backpack

A frog.
A flag.
A hot dog.
A bag.
A rock from the creek.
A sandwich from last week.
A secret map to find gold.
An orange pumpkin you can hold.
The wing of a bee.
Seeds I got for free.

If I dig deep,
there are *more* things I'd like to keep!
A zipper from a tent.
A card my sister sent.
A hinge off an old gate.
The bag from some chips I ate.
A page from a song.
A rubber band that's strong.

I'm glad I have a large backpack!

SEED

Pumpkin and the Kitten

MILK

Pumpkin was a pet cat. He had orange stripes and sharp teeth like a tiger, but there was not a wild bone in him.

Pumpkin did not have to hunt for his supper, and he never felt a twinge of hunger. He did not have to hide from dogs or live in a barn. He had a safe home and lots of snacks. Nick and Kate met his needs.

Pumpkin was glad to be a pet cat.

Pumpkin had the best places to sleep.

He slept on the porch in the sun.

He slept in a basket in the shade.

He slept in square boxes.

He slept in soft laps.

No place was off limits.

Pumpkin had catnip to find and fake mice to chase. He had yarn to shred. Pumpkin made up fun games for himself like "Hide and Seek," "Bat the Bed Fringe," and "Swing on the Drapes."

He had time to push paperclips and pencils off the desk and see them roll. And he did not have to share a thing.

Life was sweet …

… until the morning that Pumpkin woke up from a nap and Nick had a kitten in his arms. It was a big shock to Pumpkin. Nick put the kitten in a box with a blanket, and Kate put a dish of milk by her.

Kate said, “Pumpkin, she can be your sister! She is a cute kitten.”

But Pumpkin did not think that was true. A plan came into his mind to rid himself of the kitten.

I will just pretend she is not here.

Then I will hiss at her and make her see that I am in charge.

I will bare my large teeth at her.

I will chase her and make her run fast.

I will scare her until she hides.

I will bite her and make her cry. I will make her wish she never came. Then, at last, I will be rid of her.

Nick said, “Pumpkin, stop it! I see your glare! You be kind to the kitten! Understand?”

Pumpkin did not understand.

"You will like her after a while," Kate said.

Pumpkin stared at her.

Kate gave Pumpkin a pat. "Give it time. And remember that we are still your pals."

On stiff legs, Pumpkin left to take a nap on the porch.

It got cold on the porch after a while, but Pumpkin still sat there. His legs felt like ice, but he didn't even go in for supper.

Pumpkin did not forgive Nick and Kate. He gave himself a short bath and then went back to sleep, still mad.

In his sleep, Pumpkin began to feel less cold. It was like he had a thick blanket on his back. It felt nice!

Then he woke up with a jolt. The kitten was in bed with him. It was the kitten that made him feel less cold.

Pumpkin was torn. *Do I scold her for this, or do I act like she is not here?*

OK. The kitten can share the bed with me for a short time.

Pumpkin forgot to be mad.

He even gave the kitten a lick.

The kitten woke up and gave him a lick back.

And Pumpkin forgave Nick and Kate and the kitten.

The End

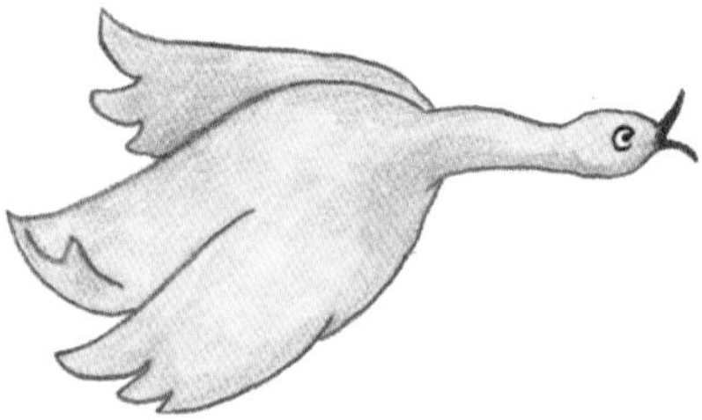

Oh, Brother!

This is Brother. He lives on a farm with Grandmother.

Do you see Brother's big grin? When he grins like that, it's a clue that he is up to his tricks. But he will never admit it! If you ask him what he's up to, he will yell, "Nothing!"

Uh-oh, here comes Grandmother.

Brother has a big grin on his face. He runs to get his gloves. When Brother gets to the front gate, Grandmother stares.

Oh, Brother!
What's the matter?
I have my gloves on.

You see? I told you that big grin was a clue. Let's see what other tricks Brother will do.

Brother runs here and there. What will he put in his bucket? He grabs leftover pancakes, fish, milk, and one bag of nuts.

Uh-oh. There's that big grin.
Brother, what are you up to?

You can bet that with Brother,
"nothing" is "something."

And what is under that cover? It's cheese! The pigs do a jig.

But here comes Grandmother. She stops and stares.

Brother's tricks have made the pigs glad, but not Grandmother.

Did Brother do the job well? Not if you ask Grandmother.

Brother, you got slop on the geese! I like my geese to be white. Rinse the geese—and no tricks this time!
Yes, Grandmother.

Brother gets the hose.

Uh-oh. What's that on Brother's face? Yes, it's a big grin. What do you think he'll do? Let's ask.

Brother, what are you up to?

Do you trust Brother?
Will Grandmother?

Here she comes. She stops and stares.

Is Grandmother mad? Or is that a smile on her face? It's hard to tell.

This time Brother gets his chores done. And then it's time for lunch and cake!

But where is Grandmother? Brother yells for her.

Grandmother, can you ice the cake so we can have some?
Grandmother?

Grandmother, what is in that bucket?

Hold on. Is that a big grin on Grandmother's face? Grandmother, what are you up to?

Brother stares.

The End

Cricket's Picnic

Springtime came to Pepper Park
and Cricket had a plan.
"I'll have a picnic for my pals!"
And then the fun began.

He grated cheese and cut up leeks
and shaped them into tarts.
He got a plate to shell the nuts,
then chopped them into parts.

As he cracked and whisked the eggs
for plum and nutmeg cake,
old Fly buzzed by to take a taste—
"Stop! It has to bake!"

When Chipmunk came to see the fun,
he sat and licked his lips
as Cricket added spices to
the cups of acorn dip.

Then sweet Rabbit scampered from
his home deep in the grove.
He sniffed the cider in the pot
that simmered on the stove.

Cricket blended. Cricket mixed.
He had so much to do!
He made muffins, cakes, and tarts
until his face was blue!

Chipmunk, Fly, and Rabbit chattered,
"We can help you, Cricket!
But ... before you rinse the silverware,
will you let us lick it?"

They danced and sang a picnic song
as they prepared the lunch:
"Crackers, jam, and buttermilk!
Yum, yum—MUNCH!"

They filled a basket to the top
with yum-yums they had made,
then marched off to the picnic spot
and set up in the shade.

Bullfrog, Snake, and Robin came.
Spider was there, too.
Cricket smiled and said, "I'm glad
to share these yums with you."

"What's nicer than a picnic lunch
with nothing to upset us?"
Then he danced a cricket dance
and passed the plate of lettuce.

The End

Life on *The Blue Whale*

This is the tale of my life on a shrimp ship called *The Blue Whale*.

I used to spend the summers as a deckhand. I scrubbed the decks, steered the ship, peeled the spuds, and shined the trim.

I liked life on the ship.

I still remember …

… the smell of the water.

… the waves that rocked me to sleep.

… the call of the gulls in the morning.

… the shrimp net on the deck.

… the feel of the wind on my face.

The Blue Whale

One summer was better than all the rest.

What happened, you ask?

Here is the tale that I will never forget.

The ship was far from shore. There was no land to be seen.

In the mornings, a whale swam next to us. She was never far from the ship. This is why we called the ship *The Blue Whale*.

One morning, something changed.

The whale swam up to the ship. A crab and a starfish clung to her back! They hopped off onto the deck of the ship.

The crab jumped into a pile of rope. The starfish spun and danced a jig. My shipmates and I liked to see them scamper and slide on the wet deck.

The two critters seemed quite at home on the ship.

This went on for more than a week. We all had fun.

Then the sky got dark and a big storm swept in!

The wind raged. Waves rocked the ship back and forth. Water splashed onto the deck.

The crab and the starfish clung to my leg. I rushed to steer the ship.

I pushed the wheel hard to the left, but the wind was too strong.

By the time the storm was over, the ship was off track.

I pulled the map from the shelf by the washstand. The crab and the starfish sat next to me, and we stared at the map for a long time.

NW
NE
W
E
SW
S
SE

I put the ship back on track and went north.

The crab and the starfish helped. We made it!

The end of summer came. It began to get colder.

Then one brisk morning, the whale swam close up to the ship. My chums hopped off the deck and onto her back.

As the three of them drifted off, my shipmates and I waved and called after them. "So long! So long!"

It was time for us to go home as well.

I will never forget that summer with the crab and the starfish on *The Blue Whale.*

The End

Wild Rice Harvest

In the fall, we sat by a campfire on the shores of Finger Lake. Dad carved an old stick.

Dad told us that there were rice beds not far from the campsite. He had harvested wild rice there as a boy.

We had never harvested wild rice before, so we asked him to tell us more.

This is what he told us.

Wild rice is a kind of grass seed. The seed is long and black. It ripens in the fall.

The wild rice plant lives in lakes and ponds.

The plant likes full sun and rich, moist soil.

Ducks feed on the seed. Muskrats and deer enjoy the entire plant.

Wild rice is gathered by hand, and the best time to gather it is in the fall.

The ripe rice falls off the plant when you tap it.

It takes a while to gather even a small bit of rice.

After the harvest, the rice must be prepared.

Here are the steps:

Cure the rice.
Put the rice on a sheet. Let the sun dry it.

Thresh the rice.
Dig a small pit and line it with the sheet. Put the rice into the pit and step on it. The chaff (the thin shell of the rice) will fall off.

Toss the rice.
The chaff will fly off in the wind.
The wild rice will fall back into the pan.

Store the rice.

Put it in jars or bags and it will keep a long time. If it is kept dry, the rice will not spoil.

Dad finished his tale. He pulled a small bag of wild rice from his backpack. We boiled a pot of water on the campfire and made wild rice for supper.

If you like, you can make it too!

Hot Wild Rice

1. Boil 4 cups of water or chicken broth.
2. Add 1 cup of wild rice and 1 cup of white rice.
3. Simmer until the rice is tender and the kernels puff open. Fluff the rice with a fork. Add a pat of butter.

Enjoy!

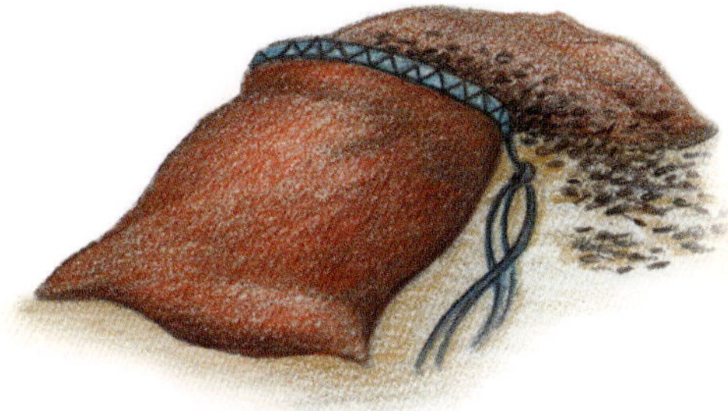

The End

Rawhide

My name is Rawhide. I'm a ranch dog. I'm the boss of this place. I protect the kids and keep things in order.

Mr. and Mrs. August drove off in the truck. They left me in charge of the kids. There is a ranch hand, but he's not much help.

While the kids have pancakes, I go for a short stroll.

I spot a large rat by the sawmill. I chase it over a pile of sawdust. He won't be back while I'm on the job.

SAWMILL

I dust off my paws and go on with my tasks.

Did the cat just drink from the fish pond? That will not do!

I bark at the cat to scold her. She ignores me, so I make her go back to the barn. That won't happen twice!

The ranch hand enters the chicken pen. I crawl over to spy on him. Did he just nab an egg? I'll put a stop to that!

I creep over the straw and jump at him. He drops his basket and flees.

The kids are on the lawn in bare feet. I see a huge green snake coiled up by the seesaw.

I pause ... then I jump onto the wild snake and haul it off. I have saved the kids!

Just then, the truck chugs up the lane. Mr. and Mrs. August step out—but who is with them?

They call her Aunt Sue, and she has a blue shawl. Her arms are filled with boxes and bags. This upsets me!

I have never seen her before, but the kids seem to like her. I don't understand why!

The kids take the boxes from her. Stop! I have not checked the boxes yet to see if they are safe!

Aunt Sue sets a box in front of me and opens it. It smells like bacon. I love bacon!

Perhaps she isn't as bad as she seems. In fact, I love Aunt Sue!

We all go inside to wash up for supper. I sprawl on my bed while Mrs. August makes the sauce.

I am tired. Yawn!

I must rest up so I can start over in the morning.

The End

Queen Bee

Queen Bee sat on her throne. She gazed at the flowers outside her hive. She was sad.

Queen Bee said to herself,

"Spring has sprung
and there is so much to see …
hills of green
and bugs that fly free.

But here I am,
a sad queen bee.
I'm stuck in this hive,
and I want to flee!"

Yes, it was true. Queen Bee did not want to be queen of the hive any more.

You see, Princess Dragonfly had told her of life outside the hive. Queen Bee did not want to miss it.

So when it got dark, she left her crown on her bed. Then she crept out of her hive without a sound.

Queen Bee set off to find Princess Dragonfly.

She found the princess down by the river bank.

"Hello, Princess Dragonfly!

You've been north and south
and all the rest.
Which thing do you think
is the best?"

Princess Dragonfly said, "I think that owls are the best things. You must see one!"

And so Queen Bee set off to find an owl.

Brown Owl was in a deep sleep in his tree. Queen Bee made a loud buzz with her wings.

The owl woke up and blinked.

Queen Bee said,

"Hello, Brown Owl!

You've been north and south
and all the rest.
Which thing do you think
is the best?"

Brown Owl said,

"I think that fire is the best thing. Fire can last all winter long and never get cold."

Then the owl yawned and went back to sleep.

Queen Bee went to find fire. She found it in a ring of stones at a campground.

"Hello, Mr. Fire!

You've been north and south
and all the rest.
Which thing do you think
is the best?"

Mr. Fire said,

"Trees are the best things.
I cannot live without them!"

Queen Bee thanked Mr. Fire and
set off to find the trees.

Queen Bee found an old elm tree in the forest.

She said,

"Hello, Big Elm!

You've been north and south
and all the rest.
Which thing do you think
is the best?"

The old tree said,

"Flowers are the best things. They cover the ground like a carpet of stars. Flowers are what I like most!"

Queen Bee set out to find flowers.

She saw a crowd of wildflowers under the tree. She landed on them and said,

"Hello, Wise Wildflowers!

You've been north and south
and all the rest.
Which thing do you think
is the best?"

The wildflowers smiled and said,

“The best things we’ve ever seen are bees! They help all of us. We need bees!”

Queen Bee smiled a big, big smile.

"Thank you, Wildflowers!
You're so wise, I can see.
And now I'll fly back ...
to my hive and my bees!"

The helper bees were glad to see Queen Bee. They asked her where she had been.

Queen Bee said,

"I've seen so much, from north to south—
the trees and all the rest.
I now understand my life with you
is better than the best!

My bees, I hope you will forgive
my sadness and my frowns.
My place is with you in this hive ...
I'm glad to keep my crown!"

Then Queen Bee sat on her throne and smiled. She was home.

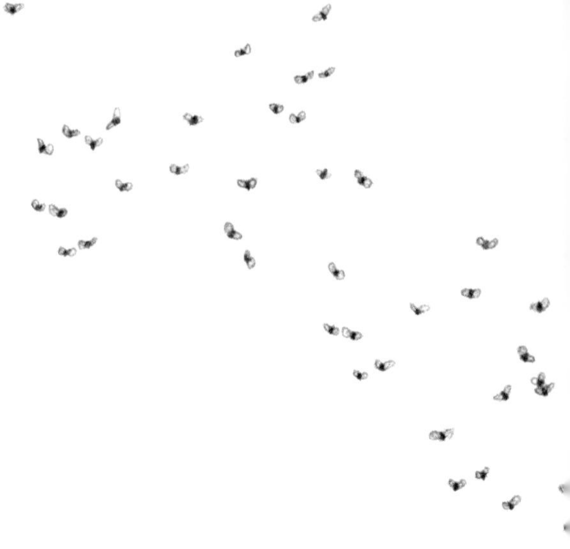

The End

Are you ever scared
to flip the page
and find out that there is ...

no more
to read?

(It's OK!
Go on to Level 3!)